I love Notre Dame because my dad, brother, and uncle went there. I can't wait to go there, too.

Future Domer Connor, age 10

The best thing about Notre Dame is the Grotto. I love going to the Grotto and lighting a candle for my family.

Future Domer Sophia, age 9

Notre Dame is the most special place in the world because the campus always gives me a special feeling.

Future Domer Christian, age 10

First Edition
ISBN 0-9766552-0-9

Designed by Allison Walsh

Printed by Ave Maria Press, Notre Dame, IN
Printed in the United States of America

FUTURE DOMERS

A Child's Guide to Notre Dame

Written by Sharon Bui ND '02, '04

Illustrated by Future Domers – Children and students
who aspire to attend school beneath the Golden Dome:

Kathleen, age 12

Sarah, age 11

Thomas, age 10

Stephanie, age 11

Geneva, age 10

Kristopher, age 11

Elizabeth, age 16

Foreword

Students, Alumni, and Friends of Notre Dame:

I feel blessed and humbled to have the opportunity to introduce you to the book "Future Domers," as it is our young generation that will allow us to continue to nurture Notre Dame in its most sincere and dynamic form. Sharon Bui shares the gift of our University beautifully as she embraces the Notre Dame family as her own. Deeply rooted in service, Sharon possesses a tremendous amount of enthusiasm and passion for helping others in need. As a member of the Class of 2002 and as a graduate of the Alliance for Catholic Education, she was a source of Irish pride among her peers, including being named as the "Super Fan" by our student newspaper, The Observer, her senior year. Beyond her spirit, Sharon believes strongly in living the mission of God and in Notre Dame. Whether one finds her in solemn prayer at the Grotto or singing the Notre Dame fight song, it is inevitable that she will infect you with her passion for Our Lady's University.

I trust that you will find it within your spirit and embrace in your heart the themes of these pages. Just as Sharon has eloquently depicted the sense of place that is Notre Dame, importance lies for each of us to spread the goodwill and compassionate spirit of this University to others. The Notre Dame experience is about faith, love, and a desire to extend our gifts to others. Perhaps each of you will become inspired to make someone else's life more meaningful through your own actions, most hopefully the lives of children. May God's peace bless each of you in the most profound and deepest way always.

May I say in closing, I am enormously proud of Sharon Bui, one of our outstanding graduates. May her good work continue.

Ever devotedly in Notre Dame,

Father Ted Hesburgh, c.s.c.

(Rev.) Theodore M. Hesburgh, C.S.C.
President Emeritus

The University of Notre Dame has a beautiful campus in Notre Dame, Indiana. A Catholic priest named Father Edward Sorin founded the school in 1842. Many students say Notre Dame is a magical place.

The Golden Dome is one of the most famous university landmarks in the world. The Golden Dome is on the main building on campus. A 19-foot statue of Notre Dame, which means "Our Lady," stands on top of the Golden Dome. Our Lady is the mother of Jesus. She watches over the entire campus and all who visit.

The Irish Guard is a group of 10 students dressed in kilts. They always march in front of the band. The Irish Guard has a tradition of leading band members across campus and into Notre Dame Stadium on football Saturdays. Students must be at least 6 feet 2 inches tall to try out for the Irish Guard.

Notre Dame has the oldest university band in the land. Students are excited when they hear the band play the Notre Dame Victory March. The Notre Dame tradition of cheering and supporting the football team is unlike the tradition of any other school. Notre Dame has fans from all over the United States and from around the world. Thousands of fans gather to cheer the Irish onward to victory.

Notre Dame football players work hard to become better athletes and earn good grades in the classroom. The student section is always excited to cheer on their classmates, win or lose. Students are proud to shout "WE ARE ND" and "GO IRISH!" At the end of every game, Irish players raise their golden helmets to thank fans.

Students work on projects and study for tests at Hesburgh Library. The library is named after Father Theodore Hesburgh, who was president of the University from 1952 to 1987. Father Hesburgh played an important role in helping Notre Dame excel as an outstanding school for studying, growing in faith, and succeeding in sports. A colorful mural of Jesus with open arms reminds students that He is always watching over them. The mural is nicknamed "Touchdown Jesus" because his open arms look like He is signaling a touchdown in football.

Students enjoy living in the dorms with their friends. A dorm is a building in which students live together during college. In the dorms, students become a part of the Notre Dame family. Roommates and friends share many memories. Every dorm on campus has a chapel where students can gather and pray with their friends.

A basilica is a beautiful and important church recognized by the Pope who is head of the Catholic Church. The words "God, Country, Notre Dame" are written above the entrance door of the Basilica of the Sacred Heart. These words hold a special meaning for the students of Notre Dame. Notre Dame students feel it is important to share their faith and use their talents to help others. Many students participate in service projects in different parts of the country and world.

The Grotto honors Notre Dame, Our Mother. Students can light a candle and pray for their family and friends. The Notre Dame Grotto is one-seventh of the size of the actual Grotto in Lourdes, France, where the Virgin Mother appeared to St. Bernadette. A special statue of Our Mother reminds visitors that she is always present.

Notre Dame graduates are called Domers. Domers are proud of their time at the University of Notre Dame. Each moment spent on campus is a blessing. Even though graduates may leave the University, they are members of the Notre Dame family forever. Remember to study hard and pray daily so that one day you, too, can become a Domer.

GO IRISH!

Acknowledgements

Special thanks to my parents, Ty and Kim Bui, for helping me achieve my dream of going to Notre Dame. Without their prayers, love, and financial support, I would have never been able to soak in the many blessings beneath the Golden Dome. Thank you to my sisters, Kimberly and Katie, and my brother Dominic for always making me laugh and for having patience with me when listening to the countless hours I brag about Notre Dame. Huge thanks to my grandparents, aunts, and uncles who have always provided me with encouragement. To my SMS girls – Caroline Baldwin, Katie Maughan, and Rebekah Walker – your friendship and advice mean so much to me. To Sister C and my Farley girls, thanks for being my second family from the very first day I arrived on campus. Special thanks to Allison Walsh for assisting me with the layout. Thanks to Matt Daily, Adam Russ, Andrew Gawrych, and Scott Ford for innovative suggestions. To all my students, you continue to inspire me with your hard work and creativity. You will always hold a special place in my heart. To Melissa Kalas and family, Kaylea Hoelscher, and Tim Dolezal, I dream of the day that we will have ND tailgates side-by-side. To the Notre Dame family, ACE friends, ushers, Professor Jim McKenna, Center for Social Concerns, members of the Congregation of Holy Cross, Padre Don McNeill C.S.C., Sue Cunningham, Dean Jennifer Nemecek, the Andrews and McMeel families, Father Bill Miscamble C.S.C., Marcie Sandleben, Steve Camilleri, the Leep family, and fellow Domers, my Notre Dame experience would have never been complete without you. To Father Ted Hesburgh C.S.C., thank you for your words of inspiration and dedication to the Notre Dame family. Thanks to Father Edward Sorin C.S.C. for establishing the best university on earth. Last but not least, thanks to Our Lord and Our Mother, Notre Dame for always listening and answering my prayers.

God bless and GO IRISH!

Sharon Bui

Sharon Bui